GOLD PANNING EQUIPMENT, BUILD YOUR OWN

MITCHELL WAITE

DEDICATION

TO MY FATHER, JERRY. HE TOUGHT ME TO
LOVE THE OUTDOORS AND TO APPRECIATE
THE FINER THINGS OF NATURE.

CONTENTS

INTRODUCTION

A wise old prospector once said, "If you think it's gold, it isn't." This comes from the fact that gold is all by itself when it comes to natural properties and is easily recognizable in its pure form "free gold". It is heavy and it sticks out in the pan with a few exceptions. Gold will float on water tension, and it is hard to recognize when it is held in state with other minerals.

Let's take the first statement—gold floats on water tension. Yes, it does. The old timers tell you to never to touch the inside of a dry pan because it leaves oils from your hand on the pan itself. This oil will cause the gold to float out of the pan along with the other debris. To stop this, many experienced gold panners "burn" their pans on a regular basis. The burning rids the pan of oil. Burn their pans? Of course, I am talking about metal gold pans. Not the plastic. They simply toss the metal pan on the fire and let it get good and hot. Afterwards, they will pour water in it and let it rust. The a dark brown rusty pan will help the gold to stand out during panning. In fact, I was once told by 'Vic the Panner', "The rustier the pan the better. The pan gets full o' little holes an' rust pits where the gold wedges into when ya back wash the pan." So what about those plastic pans? Just wash them out very well with dish soap. Make sure you rinse them to the point where there is no sign of soap.

You have to be the most careful with floating gold when you are panning and back-washing the black sand. If you let the gold become dry and then hit it with water, the oils come into play and the gold will float. If this happens, just touch the gold with a finger and it will instantly sink. The second statement about gold being hard to recognize when mixed with other minerals. This is also true. Since it is not in it's pure form, it changes appearances. For instance, the gold from Cripple Creek, Colorado. Cripple Creek is one of the biggest gold producing areas in the United States. Hard rock mining methods are used to remove the gold from deep within the earth. The ore is a grayish color and one would never guess, off hand, that there was gold within the matrix.

Perhaps, that is one reason the Cripple Creek gold rush days were late in getting started. It was well after the gold rush to Sutter's Mill in California, that someone finally discovered the gold in Cripple Creek. It turned out to be one of the biggest producing areas world wide.

In this book we will keep our discussions to "Free Gold". That gold which is found free of any supporting matrix or debris. Free gold will be somewhere in the neighborhood of 23 Karats pure and may be found in placer deposits. We will not be concerned with veins, shafts, or hard rock mining.

With free gold, you will know when it is gold. It will have a low shining luster and lay in the crease of your pan. When you see it, you will know it.

CHAPTER 1: THE PROPERTIES OF GOLD AND HELPFUL HINTS

In order to understand how the equipment you are building works, you need to know a little about gold and it's properties. I won't bore you with the scientific data such as atomic weights etc, but more about where it is found, how it can be identified, and how different pieces of equipment work better than others.

Gold is usually associated with quartz when it is in vein type deposits. It may appear as wires, flakes, nuggets and alloys. Free gold is usually in an alluvial deposit mixed with various sands, gravel, dirt, or mud. Gold is found almost everywhere, but some amounts are easier to work than others. In fact, gold is number 58 in the order of abundance of the elements found in the crust of the earth.

The different alloys or combinations of gold cause an appearance change. Gold from California has a deeper yellow luster than that of Colorado. And, Arizona gold is even lighter than the two. This is mostly due to the impurities found in each (such as silver). It is interesting to note that gold in its natural form has a "finger print" to which the origin can be traced. Yes, gold from one mine can be distinguished from another. Assayers can even identify from which state or district the gold came from. Of course, this is only true if the gold has not been refined to a pure state.

Gold is almost always associated with silver. When in this state, it is referred to as electrum. It also occurs with various other metals and minerals such as lead, mercury, sulfur, antimony pyrites, galenas, etc. Therefore, if you find a good source of "Fool's Gold", don't throw it away. Many of the "Old Timers" threw away their fortune because they figured it to be worthless. Instead, have that fool's gold assayed! Besides, many a rock hound will now pay good money for a good chunk of the stuff.

Gold can also be found in the ocean. It is usually mixed at a 5 to 250 parts in 1,000,000 gallons of water. Some estimates have been made as to how much gold there is in the ocean, and it is quite astounding. Would you believe somewhere in the neighborhood of 200 billion tons?

The problem here is figuring out a cost effective recovery system. Some people have come up with some interesting systems to collect all that gold. One such system utilizes Red Plankton. Red Plankton collects and maintains gold within its microscopic bodies. If the plankton could be successfully farmed, one might have a good producing gold mine. Unfortunately, Red Plankton only grows at certain depths and temperatures in the ocean. Conditions have to be exact for the plankton to grow.

Gold in its pure state, is the most malleable and ductile of all the metals. When you find a sample, which appears to be near pure, you should be able to dent the metal with your fingernail. It will not flake or break. It is soft like lead. Back in the old days, the way to tell a pure gold coin was to bite it. If you couldn't leave a dent in the coin from your teeth, then it wasn't pure gold. In the field there is another good test to perform. The scratch test is simple yet very effective. Simply take a sharp object such as a pocket knife and scratch your sample. If it flakes and seems hard, it is not pure gold. You should get a clean groove with possible peals of metal. If you want something to practice on, try a section of lead. It acts the same way.

Another thing to keep in mind. Gold is bright yellow and has a high luster except when it comes in very fine particles. Fine gold, like other powders, appears black. Sometimes it will appear as a purple or dark blue grain.

An interesting story to illustrate this point is when I was once given the offer by a placer mine owner to work his mine. His offer was for me to work his claim, and I could keep all of the gold that I could see as long as I turned over all of the black sand from my panning efforts. He finally told me why he was willing to make such an offer. Only 10% of the gold is visible. The rest is hidden in the black sand. DON"T throw away your black sand!

The removal of gold from the black sand can be done either mechanically or by chemicals. The mechanical method involves magnets to extract the black sand. Most of the black sand is iron ore, and will stick to a magnet. Since gold is non magnetic, it will not be picked up by the magnet. However, the smaller particles may be trapped between the black sand particles. To keep this from happening, keep the black sand or gold concentrates submerged in water while the magnet is moved around in the pan.

A hint about using the magnet—place a piece of plastic over the magnet before dipping it into the black sand. Then all you have to do to clean the black sand off the magnet is remove the plastic. When doing this procedure do not use a metal pan. You won't get all of the black sand out of your concentrates.

Gold is extremely inactive and is unaffected by air, heat, moisture, and most solvents. But, it will dissolve in bromides, chlorides, and some iodides. Other dissolving agents are alkali cyanides, aqua regia, and it will be held in an amalgam state by mercury. BEWARE! These chemicals can be deadly if handled improperly.

The mercury is a method, which works well to remove all those tiny particles of gold in your black sand. Place a drop of mercury in the pan and swish it around until it has had an opportunity to contact all the materials in the pan. When done remove the mercury and put it back into a bottle for use at a later time. The purpose of this is to use the mercury until it is saturated with gold. You can tell it is saturated because it will move slowly and seem much more dense than before.

To clean the gold out of the mercury, you can use a thin chamois cloth. Place the mercury in the chamois and wring the mercury out. The gold will be stuck in the chamois, and you can use the mercury again. Again, BEWARE—to not let your skin come in contact with the mercury. Wear a good pair of rubber gloves for protection.

Another method of removing the gold from the mercury the use of a large syringe and cotton balls. This method involves placing wet cotton balls into the syringe by pressing them with the plunger until they are pressed into a filter. The mercury is then put into the syringe (after removing the plunger). The plunger is replaced and the mercury is forced through the cotton filter. The filter is then removed and processed to remove the gold. The mercury that comes out of the syringe is reused again and again.

4

Now to get the gold out of the chamois or the cotton ball filter, cut out the piece which strained the mercury or remove the cotton filter and place it in a crucible. Pour some nitric acid on it and it will dissolve and leave behind your gold. Make sure you do this in a well ventilated area because the fumes from the nitric acid and left over mercury are toxic and could be fatal if inhaled.

THE AUTHOR TRYING NEW TECHNIQUES

CHAPTER 2: WHY GOLD PANNING?

No matter what method you use to concentrate your placer gold, you will find it is necessary to pan the concentrates to finish the operations.   Therefore, panning must be mastered. Keep in mind, gold will be the heaviest particles in the pan. It is 19 times heavier than any thing else in the pan.   It will settle to the bottom very quickly if the dirt is agitated; especially, if the materials are suspended in water.   This is the basis for all panning methods from the slice box to the dredge and even the pan.

The simplest method of mining gold is panning. This involves a circular dish shaped object with a fold or crease around the bottom. The old timers sometimes used frying pans and pie tins. Today, the pans come in metal or plastic and the bottom of the pans are flat. The edge is usually at a 45 degree angle from the bottom. Some modern pans have gold traps and riffles to help keep the gold from floating out of the pan.

So if panning is so effective, why not pan everything? That becomes evident with the following example:

Given: You have a parcel of ground, which contains an ounce of gold per twelve cubic yards. This is about average for most placer mines.

A person using a 14 inch pan (assuming they know what they are doing) can finish a cubic yard in an eight hour day of panning. This results in 1/12 of an ounce completed which translates to about $100 (at $1200 a Troy ounce). Panning can get pretty old at this rate. The same person using a dredge with a 2-inch intake can do 12 cubic yards in about 4 hours. At the end of 8 hours he has two ounces of gold (about $2400 worth) sitting in about one cubic foot of black sand. This is a whole lot easier to pan out, and it is about 250 times faster than panning alone.

I would like to point out that most commercial placer mines use huge "High-bankers" with rock classifiers. These large high-bankers are nothing more than an oversized sluice box with straining screens and water pumps to remove the rocks before entering the sluice. The water is pumped into the box and the material is fed into the classifiers by means of a front-loader tractor or steam shovel. In this case, the extraction process can be up to a thousand times faster than panning. The problem now becomes running out of placer deposits before you find another.

Regardless, it all boils down to panning. Therefore, the panning method is an important part of gold extraction.

CHAPTER 3: GOLD PANNING TECHNIQUES

Over the years I have tried several methods of panning and found the "Sluff" method to be the quickest and easiest to master. It also concentrates the black sand and gold in a highly efficient manner. However, you may want to try the other methods to see what fits your liking. I will not cover these other methods in this book.

The first thing to consider is the selection of your pan. The larger the pan, the more material you can process at one time. But, a larger pan is hart to handle with control and sometimes takes a toll on your arms and wrists. Consequently, the size of pan is strictly a matter of choice and what you feel comfortable handling. Does the pan need gold traps and riffles, and should it be metal or plastic?

First, traps and riffles are not necessary for the experienced panner. But, the riffles and traps give a little extra efficiency for the beginner. Metal or plastic pans both have advantages and disadvantages. Metal pans usually do not incorporate traps and riffles, but they are more durable than plastic. They do not crack after extensive use. Metal pans have to be burned on a regular basis to rid them of any oil build up from handling. This is done by tossing the metal pan on a fire until it quits smoking. Then it is ready to use after it is cooled. Plastic pans come with the traps, and as mentioned above, they do seem to crack after long periods of use. This happens more in the larger pans. Some of the advantages are the pans do not have to be burned to get rid of the oil on your hands. The metal pans do. The plastic pans can be washed with a good dish detergent instead. Now that you have selected your pan, let's use it. Step 1. The Shake Down. Fill the pan to one third capacity. Over filling does not help efficiency or speed. Place enough water into the pan to completely cover the dirt even after the dirt has been saturated. Squish through the dirt to ensure all particles are wet and there are no dry clods or clay pockets. Pick out any rocks from the pan (making sure each has been washed off while in the pan).

Orient the pan to where the riffles are away from you and the pan is level. With a hand on each side of the pan, shake the pan from side to side vigorously at least twenty five times. This motion will allow the gold to settle to the bottom of the pan. If the dirt is muddy or has a lot of clay, you may have to shake it twice as much. Do not use any forward, backward, or circular motions. This will only serve to move your gold away from the riffles.

A WEATHER BEATEN
PLASTIC PAN

THE PROPER WAY TO HOLD A PAN

At this point the gold is sitting on the bottom of the pan. Do not sluff any debris off at this point because you have to work the gold into the crease (or trap) of the pan. This is done by the "Tilt Shake." Step 2. The Tilt Shake. This step is accomplished by transitioning from the shake down to a tilted pan while shaking. You stop tilting the pan when the gravel is about to fall out of the pan. When you have reached this point, cease increasing the tilt, but continue to shake for at least as many shakes as you did in the shake down. The tilt should be away from you.

At this point the gold has moved down the bottom of the pan to the crease (or trap). It's now time to do the "Sluff." Step 3. The Sluff. With the pan still tilted and the gravel nearly to fall out, dip the pan into a still pool of water. Any current in the pool may ruin the sluff. Therefore, a wash tub would be the perfect situation.

Once the gravel is submerged, raise the pan quickly out of the water with a slight forward motion. This technique will cause the lighter debris to sluff out of the pan into the pool of water. Repeat the motion again (no more than twice).

A GOOD PLACE TO DIG

Place more water in the pan and tilt it back toward you slightly. Follow this procedure, complete the tilt shake and sluff once again. Repeat these steps over until you begin to see black sand appearing in the crease. Soften the method until the black sand is the majority of material in the pan.

During the cycles, you can remove any stones out of the pan using a pair of tweezers. Keep your fingers and thumbs out of the pan as much as possible.

Now that you have reached the black sand, you will be getting close to seeing your gold. To see it and to remove it from the pan, you must do the backwash.

Step 4. The Backwash. This method varies from person to person. Some do the "Blueberry Hop" (a method perfected by an old timer called Blueberry). Others do a flat backwash (which is quick, but not necessarily a good way to extract all of your gold). The method I prefer is the "Tailing method".

The tailing method involves placing enough water in the pan to be able to rinse the black sand by tilting the pan in a circular counter clockwise notion. A small wave is created which will follow the crease in the bottom of the pan. This small wave will wash the black sand around the edge of the pan and will leave the gold in the crease of the pan. It will appear on the front edge where the water strikes the black sand first.

When a piece of gold is found, carefully move it to a clean part of the pan with some tweezers. You may have to swirl some water over it to get any remaining black sand away so that you can pick it up. But, be careful because you can cause the chunk of gold to float if you allow it to dry out before hitting it with the water. There are several methods of picking up your gold. One method is to use a snuffer bottle or eye dropper. You simply suck it up and squirt it into your gold container.

The second method is the use of tweezers. I find this frustrating and tedious. But, the tweezers are great for removing the smaller pebbles from the black sand.

The simplest method to remove gold is your fingers. All you have to do is touch the gold when it is laying in a dry part of the pan, and it will adhere to your fingers. I prefer to use my pinky finger because it is easiest to keep it dry while I use the others of other purposes. Once the gold is stuck to your finger you simply touch the gold to the water in you gold container, and it will fall off. So there you have it. A quick and dirty lesson on gold panning. Now let's get down to business and build the equipment that will make our panning efforts worthwhile.

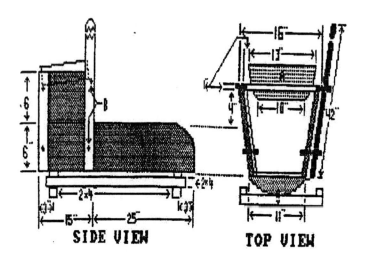

SIDE VIEW   **TOP VIEW**

CHAPTER 4: THE ROCKER

The Rocker is one of the main stays of the 'Old Time' Panning Prospector. This type of device relies on the rocking motion to help separate the free gold from the debris more efficiently than panning alone. In fact, the Rocker is 10 times faster than panning for concentrating gold, and is very good for handling gold, which may be suspended in clay.

The rocker is much like a sluice box. Both use water flow through a trough with riffles to allow the heavier gold to settle into a carpet. However, a rocker has a rounded bottom, which allows the cradle to be rocked back and forth. This rocking motion allows the dirt and clay to be agitated and the gold to fall through into the carpet. The more clay involved, the more vigorous the rocking motion is required. The Rocker is not hard to build. If made out of wood, it should be untreated pine. If made out of metal, it should be of galvanized sheet metal or aluminum. This design is for a wood rocker, but it will work as a metal design as long as the tolerances are adjusted to allow for the difference in the thickness of materials.

The Rocker consists of the Hopper, a box or trough, an apron to catch the gold, and two sets of riffles. The hopper is the initial receiver of the gold bearing gravel. It acts to screen out the larger pieces of debris such as rocks and stones larger than ¼ inch. The hopper is a box, which has a ¼ inch mesh attached to the bottom to screen the debris. This debris is guided into the first set of riffles by means of a deflector plate. Remember to inspect the rocks you remove from the hopper because they too can hold gold.

Once the gravel is dumped into the hopper, water is applied along with the rocking motion. The water may be applied through the use of a dipper or hose. (Sometimes a hose can be set up as a siphon out of an upper pool or a pump would also work nicely). However, the water should be kept as constant as possible. After a couple of rocking motions, stop for a few moments and allow the lighter debris to wash off. The smaller particles move through the screen into the first set of riffles. These riffles are designed to capture the larger pieces of gold in the Astro Turf. This Astro Turf is sandwiched into place by the riffles and the bottom of the riffle assembly. The gold will fall into the carpet just in front and back of the riffles. The smaller pieces of gold will work its way through he first set of riffles into the second set. The incline of these riffles are not as great as the first, and the water should move a little slower at this point. The smaller particles of gold will settle into the Astro Turf in these riffles. The debris will be washed off out of the end of the Rocker.

Run the rocker until black sand is visible and seems to be washing out the end of the rocker. At this point, the carpets should be pulled and washed out in a tub. The tub will catch the gold particles for further processing. Once the carpets are washed out, they can be reinstalled and returned to operation.

The washings are the gold concentrates. It is very easy to pan these concentrates and extract the gold by back washing. At the end of the season, many of the "old Timers" burn the carpets to remove the gold, which can not be removed by washing in the tubs. That is up to you.

CHAPTER 5: ROCKER ASSEMBLY
INSTRUCTIONS:

Let's start with the Hopper (listed as A in the diagram). It does not have to be a tapered box, but there should be an inch of clearance between the sides of the rocker and the hopper. This design shows the hopper as being 13" by 15" with a ¼ inch screen mounted at he bottom. Note that he hopper is not mounted level (in the profile depiction). This is to compensate for slanting the rocker. The rocker should be propped up (with rocks or blocks) to the point where the back end of the rocker is several inches higher than the front end. When this is done, the hopper should be nearly level. The easiest way to make a hopper is to use 2X4 pieces. Cut two pieces at 13 inches and two at 12 inches. Fasten the four pieces into a rectangle using 2 inch deck screws. Once the rectangle is completed, then the ¼ mesh screen can be mounted on the bottom with a heavy-duty staple gun or nails.

The deflector plate is installed next over the ¼ inch mesh to one of the 13-inch sides. This deflector plate should be made of heavy gauge metal approximately 1/8 inch thick. The sides will be bent up to direct the gravel out of the hopper into the first set of riffles. You can attach the deflector plate to the hopper using 1-inch deck screws.

The handle is easy. It is a 2" by 2" piece of wood 42 inches long. It is attached to the side of the rocker by four deck screws.

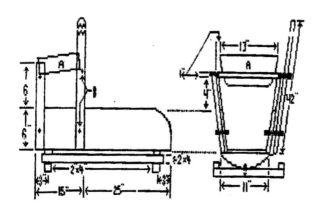

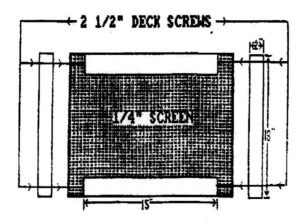

HOPPER CONSTRUCTION

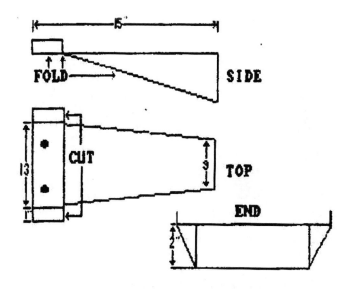

DEFLECTOR PLATE CONSTRUCTION AND INSTALLATION

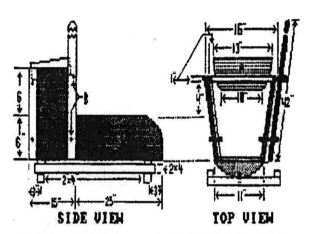

SIDE VIEW   **TOP VIEW**

B=THE ROCKER HANDLE ATTACHED TO THE SIDE BY 2 1/2" DECK SCREWS

HANDLE INSTALLATION

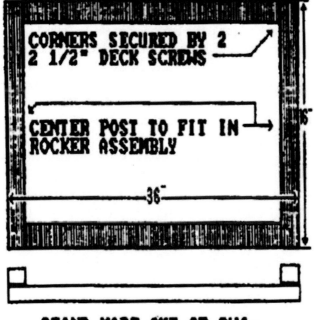

CORNERS SECURED BY 2 2 1/2" DECK SCREWS

CENTER POST TO FIT IN ROCKER ASSEMBLY

16"

36"

STAND MADE OUT OR 2X4s

STAND CONSTRUCTION AND ASSEMBLY

The stand is another easy thing to do. It is constructed out of 2 X 4 s and is used to level the cradle while in use, and to provide a platform which will keep the cradle in place while the rocking motion is applied. The cradle is kept in place by means of two pins installed in the 2 X 4 s as shown in the figure on page 24. These pins are nothing more than two-inch concrete nails hammered into the wood. The rockers are next. These too are made out of 2 X 4s. Start by cutting two pieces of wood to length (11 inches).

From this point it becomes necessary to create a pattern for the rockers. Simply take an 8 ½ by 11-inch piece of paper and fold it in half to where the paper is now showing 8 ½ by 5 ½ inches. Cut 3 ½ inches off of the 8½ length and unfold it. You should now have a 3 ½ by 11-inch rectangle. Fold it back to where it was and cut a sloping arch from the corner of one fold to halfway to the far edge.

The rockers will be attached to the bottom of the cradle by four 1 inch deck screws.

Note that holes have been drilled in the shape to allow the cement nails in the stand to move up and down freely. The holes are ½ inch in diameter.

The first set of riffles are removable and are not attached to the rocker. Since they are tapered, they will sit in the rocker at a fairly steep angle and force the gravel to the back of the rocker. You will note how the first set of riffles are a hinged assembly which allows the carpet to be held in place between the riffles and the bottom of the assembly.

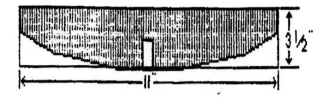

USE A 2X4 CUT AT 11". ROUND OFF
EDGES AS SHOWN, DRILL A 3/8" HOLE
IN THE CENTER FOR THE ROCKER GUIDE
POST. MAKE TWO IDENTICAL PIECES.
LEAVE ONE INCH AT THE TOP FOR
MOUNTING ON THE BOTTOM OF THE
CRADLE.

THE ROCKERS

The next step is to create the cradle. Starting with the bottom, take a 1 X 12-inch board and cut it to length at 40 inches. Set it aside for now. It will be attached to the sides and back at a latter point.

The sides are made of 1 X 6-inch boards. The two top sections are 15 inches long and the two bottom sections are 40 inches. The top and bottom sections of the cradle are attached to the side braces by means of 1½ deck screws. The side braces are pictured along with the top and bottom sections. There are 6 side braces total, and they are made out of 1 X 2-inch boards cut at 12 inches in length. Only 4 side braces will be used to secure the top and bottom sections of the sides of the cradle. The other two are used for the top and bottom sections of the back of the cradle. The back of the cradle is also made out of 1 X 6-inch boards. Cut both top and bottom sections of the back at 16 inches long. Use the last two side braces to attach the two sections together to form a 12 X 16 inch back plate. Again use 1 ½ inch deck screws fasten the pieces. Once you have a whole piece, you will need to taper the back plate. Take the back plate and decide which of the 12-inch sides will be the bottom. Along this 12-inch bottom measure 2 inches in from the each edge. Take a straight edge and make a line from the top of the back piece to the two measurements. Cut along these lines to create the tapered back plate. At this point, you are ready to create the cradle. Attach the assembled sides to the back plate.

Next, attach the bottom to the sides and back plates. The rockers and handle installation is also shown and should be accomplished at this time. The cradle is now complete, and you can set it on the stand and install the cement nails to hold it in place.

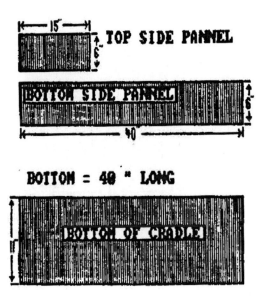

TOP SIDE PANNEL

15"

6"

BOTTOM SIDE PANNEL

6"

40"

BOTTOM = 40 " LONG

BOTTOM OF CRADLE

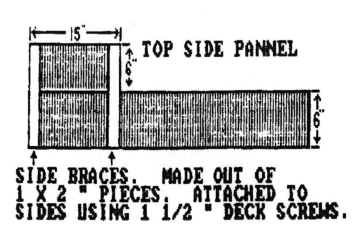

TOP SIDE PANNEL

15"

6"

6"

SIDE BRACES. MADE OUT OF
1 X 2 " PIECES. ATTACHED TO
SIDES USING 1 1/2 " DECK SCREWS.

SIDE BRACE INSTALLATION

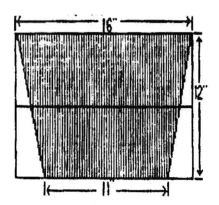

**TWO-1 X 6" PIECES CUT AS
SHOWN TO FORM THE BACK.**

BACK PLATE CONSTRUCTION

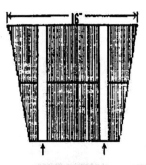

**BACK BRACES. MADE
OUT OF 1 X 2" PEICES CUT AT 12"
LONG. ATTACHED TO BACK USING
1 1/2" DECK SCREWS. THE BRACES
SHOULD BE AT LEAST 6" APPART.**

BACK BRACES

The first set of riffles is placed in the cradle. The construction is fairly simple. Again, let's start with the bottom. The bottom is made out of a 1 X 12-inch board cut at 22 inches long.

It is tapered from 12 inches at the top to 10 inches at the bottom. The riffle sides are made out of 1 X 2 inch cut at 22 inches long and are attached tot he riffles by 1½-inch deck screws. The riffles are ½ X ½ inch square dowels cut to fit the taper in the assembly at 8, 6, and 4 inches apart. A helpful hint at this point is to drill the riffles in the ends with a 1/8-inch bit to keep the dowels from splitting.

When placing the 1st riffle assembly in the cradle, make sure the riffles clear the bottom of the cradle by at least one inch. This is to allow the gravel to wash off the riffle assembly into the second set of riffles without getting clogged. There should be a free flow of material from the first set of riffles into the second. If this clearance is not obtained, place two wood blocks at the bottom of the riffle assembly to hold it up out of the cradle. These spacers are 1 X 2 X 2 inch blocks.

The Second set of riffles are attached to the cradle by a hinge in the back of the cradle assembly. This is allow for the removal of the carpet from the second set of riffles. Not shown in the drawings is a latch used to secure the opposite ends of both sets of riffles. The best thing to use is a wing nut and screw assembly to hold the riffles from opening during operations.

The second riffle assembly. Note, the assembly is not tapered and fits in the bottom of the cradle. The sides are 1 X 2 X 39 inches, and the riffles are ½ X ½ by 9 ½ inches spaced every 11 inches.

The only thing left to do is install the astro-turf in the first and second riffles, and to mount the hopper. The hopper should fit inside the cradle with some clearance between the deflector plate and the first set of riffles. If is doesn't you may have to use a bolt stock to run through the cradle from side to side to hold the hopper in the proper position.

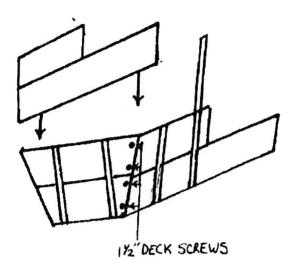

1½" DECK SCREWS

SIDES AND BACKPLATE ASSEMBLY

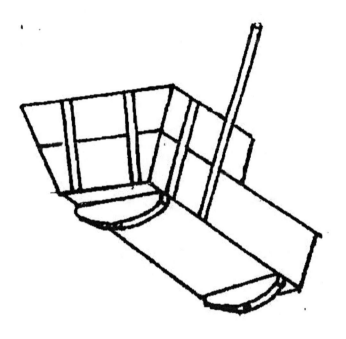

BACK AND BOTTOM ASSEMBLY WITH ROCKERS AND HANDLE

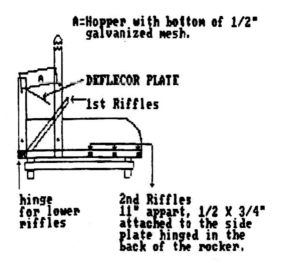

A=Hopper with bottom of 1/2" galvanized mesh.

DEFLECOR PLATE

1st Riffles

hinge for lower riffles

2nd Riffles 11" appart, 1/2 X 3/4" attached to the side plate hinged in the back of the rocker.

FIRST RIFFLE ASSEMBLY PLACEMENT

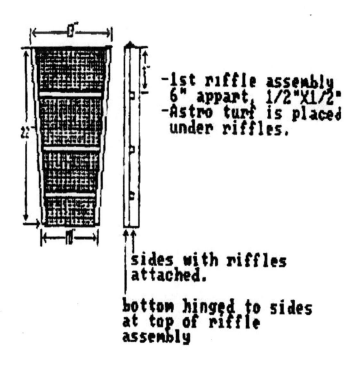

-1st riffle assembly
6" appart, 1/2"X1/2"
-Astro turf is placed
under riffles.

sides with riffles
attached.

bottom hinged to sides
at top of riffle
assembly

THE FIRST RIFFLE ASSEMBLY

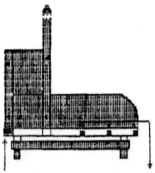

hinge
for lower
riffles

2nd Riffles
11" appart, 1/2 X 3/4"
attached to the side
plate hinged in the
back of the rocker.

SECOND RIFFLE ASSEMBLY

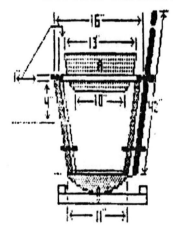

A=THE HOPPER. IT MAY BE
NECESSARY TO RUN A FRONT BRACE
ON THE OPEN END OF THE CRADLE TO
SUPPORT THE HOPPER.

CHAPTER 6: THE SLUICE BOX AND VARIOUS ADAPTATIONS

The Sluice is probably the easiest device to work large amounts of gravel. This is because several people can work the sluice at once, and there are no moving or working parts. But, water is a must. Water provides the energy to remove the gold from the gravel. In most cases, the sluice can be mounted right in the stream or a part of the stream can be diverted to the sluice. However it is done, the water has to be constant. To judge the amount of flow necessary to obtain the best results, it will be necessary to practice. However, here are some clues to work from:

For a twelve-foot sluice, there should be about a six inch difference in the elevation of the head of the sluice to the exit end.

The water should flow over all of the riffles evenly. The water should ripple over the riffles making a downward motion, which will help the gold work its way into the carpet or astro-turf. If there is no ripple, the water is flowing too fast. For this particular design, it should be about a five gallon a minute rate.

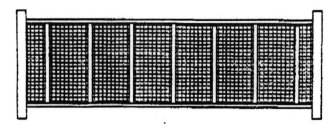

TOP VIEW

RIFFLES SHOULD BE SPACED EVENLY
(SIX TO TWELVE INCHES APPART
DEPENDING ON THE LENGTH OF THE
SLUICE). NOTE THE ASTRO-TURF
UNDER THE RIFFLES.

THE SLUICE BOX

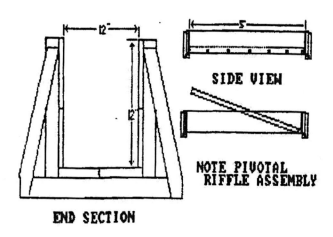

SIDE VIEW

NOTE PIVOTAL
RIFFLE ASSEMBLY

END SECTION

VIEWING THE SLUCE BOX FROM THE END

To enhance the processing of the gravel, a lead-in device may be used. Usually, it is a triangular shaped box, which acts as a funnel for the water to direct it into the Sluice. This area is also the place to sort out the bigger rocks and stones. This will also allow the riffle assembly to be extended cutting down on the receiving area. If no lead-in device is used, the receiving area will be larger and will cut down on the amount of riffles in your sluice. The sluice can be of different lengths depending upon how the gravel is suspended. The finer the gold, the longer the length should be.

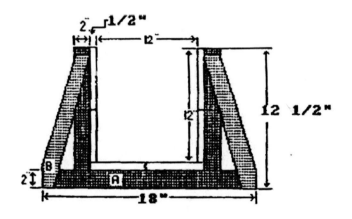

In some cases, the sluice boxes can be daisy chained together to provide the necessary length.

In this particular design, the riffles are held in place by some pivotal sides. This allow for the astro turf to be removed and washed on a regular basis. As stated above, the riffle assembly may be of different size depending upon whether or not a lead-in device is used.

Lead-in devices need not be used for daisy chained boxes, and the receiving area may also be reduced.

The sluice is a versatile piece of equipment. With a few changes, it can be turned into a dredge or a high-banker. The sluice in this book was designed to make these changes by changing the lead in device. So what's the difference between the types of equipment? Simple, they all use the sluice assembly.

A high-banker has a specific use. Many times it is impractical to transport the gold-bearing gravel to the sluice in the river or stream. Perhaps, the only source of water may be a pond. A sluice won't work. The high-banker uses some type of water delivery system to the sluice device. This system may be a gasoline powered water pump, a siphon system of hoses, or your hose in your backyard. (I sometimes go to the mountains and retrieve a load of gravel, and process it in by back yard.)

The water is pumped into the grizzly box, but you manually feed the box with gravel. This box does a rough classification of the rocks and gravel and dumps the larger items out of the box before it reaches the sluice assembly. The smaller classified gravel and gold is pumped through the sluice assembly and is processed. The gold is trapped into the carpets, and the rest of the material is expelled out of the end of the sluice assembly.

The dredge is a bit more complicated in the water and gravel delivery system. As with the high-banker, the dredge uses a grizzly box to receive the water and gravel. But, the difference is the delivery. With the dredge, you basically vacuum the bottom of the stream or lake with a nozzle and hose. The delivery system sucks up the gravel and water and pumps it to the grizzly box. The grizzly box separates the larger rocks and discards them before they enter into the sluice box.

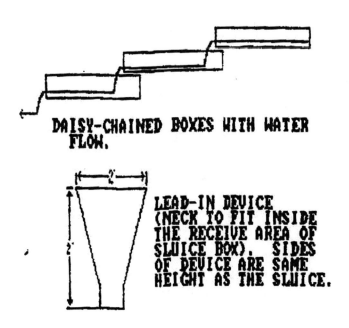

DAISY-CHAINED BOXES WITH WATER FLOW.

LEAD-IN DEVICE (NECK TO FIT INSIDE THE RECEIVE AREA OF SLUICE BOX). SIDES OF DEVICE ARE SAME HEIGHT AS THE SLUICE.

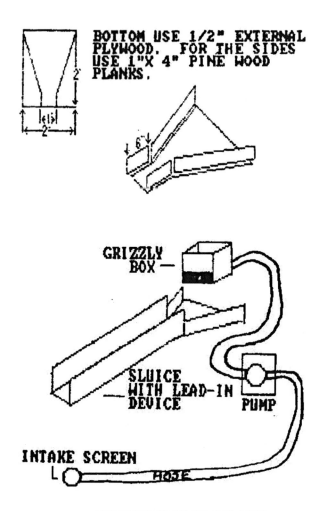

BOTTOM USE 1/2" EXTERNAL PLYWOOD. FOR THE SIDES USE 1"X 4" PINE WOOD PLANKS.

GRIZZLY BOX

SLUICE WITH LEAD-IN DEVICE

PUMP

INTAKE SCREEN

HOSE

HIGH BANKER SET UP

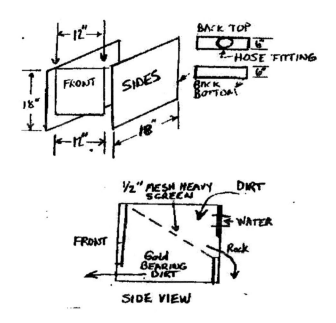

GRIZZLY BOX CONSTRUCTION

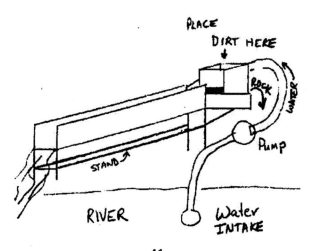

WATER AND GRAVEL FLOW THROUGH THE HIGH BANKER

The dredge has its advantages even though it is more complicated with hoses and pumping systems. These advantages are the sheer amount of dirt that can be moved through the sluice box per given time. It is also much easier to vacuum up dirt and gravel than it is to shovel it into buckets and then transport the buckets to the high-banker or sluice box.

Before using a dredge check with the local Forest Service for regulations. In some areas you may not use a dredge without filing a letter of intent to prospect a claim. In other cases, the size of dredge may be limited. In any case, check it out before setting up. You could receive a hefty fine, lose your equipment, and even receive some jail time if you break the law. We will first start with the Nozzle assembly. This will require some pipe bending, drilling, and some welding.

The first step is to obtain a two-foot section of 2-inch pipe. The pipe can be copper, brass, or mild steel. I would suggest using copper to cut down on the rust factor.

Approximately 8 inches back from one end of the pipe begin a 30-degree bend. An electrical conduit-bending device will make a nice smooth bend in the metal. Do not bend the pipe to where there is an obstruction inside the pipe caused by creases in the metal.

Directly in front of the bend of the pipe and on the 8-inch section, you will need to drill a 1 inch hole. Drilling a hole on a piece of pipe can be tricky. I suggest using a vice to hold the pipe, and a center punch to mark the spot to start drilling. This will also keep the drill bit from wandering across the pipe.

The second step is to obtain a 2-foot piece of pipe 1 inch in diameter. It should be of the same metal as the larger metal. Again, I prefer copper because welding is much

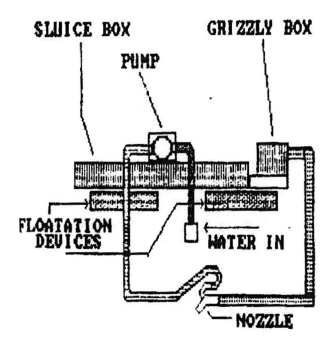

DREDGE ASSEMBLY AND SET UP

easier. In fact, instead of welding; you can soldier copper with a regular propane torch. Starting about six inches from one end of the pipe, bend it until it resembles a "U" with one side longer than the other.

Step three involves inserting the six-inch section of the 1 inch pipe into the hole made in the 2 inch pipe. Some reaming of the hold may be necessary to slide the 1 inch pipe into the 2 inch pipe.

The final step is weld the pipes into place, and the nozzle is complete. If you refer back to the dredge assembly and set up, you will see the small hose from the water pump attaches to the small pipe on the nozzle. This is the pressure hose. Water is shot through the nozzle and creates a vacuum in the 2-inch pipe.

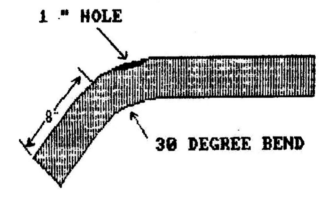

-1" PIPE BEND. THE SHORTER END WILL INSERT INTO THE 2" PIPE TO COMPLETE THE NOZZLE

ONE INCH PIPE BEND

COMPLETED NOZZLE ASSEMBLY

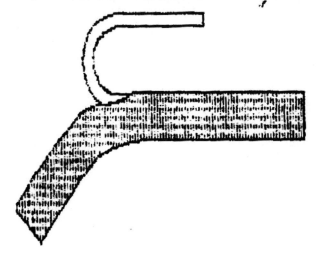

HIGH PRESSURE WATER PUMPED INTO 1" PIPE

WATER AND GOLD BEARING SAND PUSHED OUT TO GRIZZLEY BOX

SUCTION CREATED BY VENTURI

HOSES AND FLOATATION DEVICES

There are a few things I should mention about the hoses and floatation devices. The first item is the pressure hose, which runs from the pump to the nozzle on the dredge. The hose should be of good quality, which can with stand the pressure of the pump. I suggest using a 1" automotive hose or a hose, which is specifically designed to handle pressure. Pressure hoses may be found in most hardware stores which sell pool servicing equipment. The length needed depends on how deep you are willing to go when using your dredge. In most cases twenty five feet is plenty.

The next hose to discuss is the 2"hose, which extends from the nozzle to the grizzly box. This hose is a bit easier to find because it is a fairly standard swimming pool hose set up. The ribbed sides will actually help the hose from becoming kinked and plugging. The hose for the intake on the pump should resist collapsing and kinking.

The reason for this is the pump is putting a vacuum through the hose. If the hose collapses, it won't be able to pull the water to run the dredge.

The pump should deliver at least ten gallons of water a minute. It can be powered either by electrical motors or gasoline engines. I suggest sticking with the gas engines due to the potential for electrical shock and power requirements.

Floatation devices are probably the easiest to come up with. I suggest using some 15" automotive inner tubes. For stability, you may want to tie the inner tubes into pairs and lashing the tubes to a wooden platform. But, that only depends on how your are going to use your dredge. Sometimes you can get away with placing your dredge on the bank.

CHAPTER 7: THE P-TUBE

The P-tube is an easy and inexpensive tool to make which will help maximize your panning efforts. It is generally used for the final stages of removing sand and black sand from your concentrates, and it operates much like a sluice box. However, I recommend you use the P-tube at home with your water source being the garden hose. This way you can control the water flow to get the best results. The materials used in the P-tube can be purchased at your local hardware/home repair store. It consists of a section of 3-inch PCV pipe about five to six feet long and some neoprene matting.

The PCV pipe will have to be cut in half lengthwise. I suggest using a ban saw or a circular table saw with a fence that will keep the cut even.

The neoprene matting may be a bit harder to find. It is the same type of matting used on floors etc, but it must have very small ribs. The ribs should be approximately 1/8 inch apart. When you cut the neoprene, cut at a 90-degree angle to the ribs. These small ribs will act as miniature riffles like the riffles in the slice box.

When you use the P-tube, adjust the water flow to a nice even flow where no bubbles or ripples are seen. It is important to keep the flow at a steady rate.

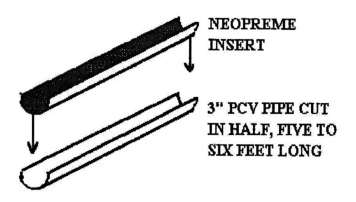

NEOPREME INSERT

3" PCV PIPE CUT IN HALF, FIVE TO SIX FEET LONG

THE 'P'-TUBE

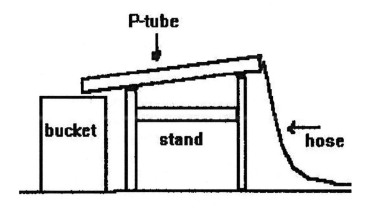

P-TUBE SET UP FOR BACK YARD USE

Use a tablespoon to feed the black sand concentrates into the P-tube. Place the sand approximately 1 foot from where the water is entering the tube. Do not move or bump the P-tube.

The visible gold will fall into the small riffles created by the ribs of the neoprene, and it will stay there. The nearly all of the sand will wash away.

As suggested before, I would use the P-tube at home in the back yard. But, care should be taken to stop the black sand from sterilizing your soil. This is easily done by putting a drain bucket under the exit of the tube. The water will fill up the bucket and overflow, but the black sand will fall to the bottom of the bucket. The water can be used to water the yard or grass. Save the black sand for further processing by the mercury process. Remember, only 10% of the gold is visible.

CHAPTER 8: GOLD TRAPS

Before you get out there and dig up an entire streambed, there are ways to simply your efforts. These are gold traps. Basically, a gold trap is a type of permanent sluice box, but is left in place (in the stream) for a year or two prior to cleaning them out.

There are two P-tube type traps. One uses PCV pipe with holes drilled in the top part. The two pieces are held apart by ½ inch spacers.

The gold travels down the top part of the tube until it falls into one of the holes and is taken out of the water flow. Another P-tube type is nothing more than corrugated pipe. The same type as what is used to drain water from one side of a road to the other. It is also referred to as a culvert.

The culvert pipe is placed in the stream to allow the gravel to flow though it. The gold is trapped in the ribs of the pipe. If you don't want to plant your own culvert trap, you can always clean out the culverts that go under the roads in gold bearing country.

Sometimes, this is the only way you can get to the pay dirt if the entire area has been claimed for mining. You can use the road right-a-way. No one can stop you from doing a public service and keeping our road culverts clean.

Other traps are basically long-term sluice boxes. Some are made out of logs, 4-inch wood blocks, and even rail road rails.

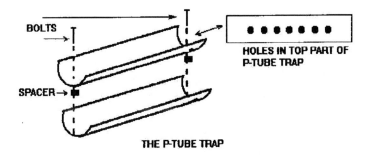

HOLES IN TOP PART OF
P-TUBE TRAP

THE P-TUBE TRAP

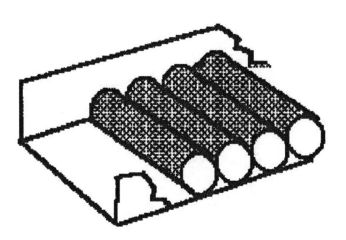

THE LOG TRAP

THE IRON RAIL TRAP
[FORTY POUND RAILS]

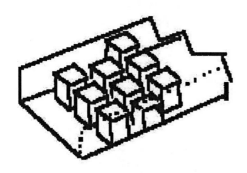

THE WOOD BLOCK TRAP

CHAPTER 9: WHERE TO GO

Once you have finished your equipment you of, course will, want to use it. There are a few things to remember while out in the field. One, be aware of all laws concerning the area you wish to hunt for gold. A good place to check is the Forest Service. The second thing to keep in mind, is most of the old gold placers were mined and turned into private land. This is done through the mining act of 1872. This can work against you or for you. If you're going to be panning on private land, you must obtain permission from the land owner prior to entering the land. If you don't, you are trespassing and can suffer the legal consequences. If you find a new source of minerals that is on state or federal land (ie a national forest) you can stake a claim using the same mining act of 1872. However, be prepared for a run around. Most government agencies will not be willing to assist you in processing your claim. Under this same law, you may also patent some of the land as your own. You'll have to check with the latest laws on this one. But, it was after seven years of working your claim you could process a title to the land. However, Congress is presently looking into changing this law. They claim they are losing too much land under this old out-dated law.

Another thing you should watch out for are claim markers. They can be a large pile of rocks or even a white post. Usually, there are markers at each corner of the claim. You want to avoid these areas. People have been shot for claim jumping.

Don't forget to obey all signs. Such as Private Property, Keep out, and No Trespassing. They usually mean it.

So where can you go where you might find a place to legally pan? I've listed some places where gold has been found in the western United States. You'll have to try to find those places where you can legally try your equipment. The places are listed by state.

ARIZONA

Alder Canyon Placers

These placers are found just north of Redington where Alder Canyon crosses the highway running south into Redington. The placers run to the west in the canyon to near Summerhaven.

Arivaca Placers

These placers are located directly north and south of Arivaca and along the highway to Oro Blanco. There is also a small placer to the east of Oro Blanco on the way to Nogales. The placer end s about five miles out of town.

Big Bug Placers

This area is along highway 69 east of Prescott between Dewey and Mayer along the Agua Fria. Most of this area is private land or claimed. Beware of the signs.

Black Canyon Placers

These placers run from Cordes to Bumble Bee southeast of Prescott along west side of highway 17. Again, this area is mostly claimed or private land. Beware.

Burro Creek Placers

These placers are located at the headwaters of both Burro Creek and
Boulder Creek just east of Bagdad. The placers extend from the junction of the two creeks up stream for about five miles. The nearest large city is Kingman to the north west.

Camp Creek placers.

These placers are just east of Cave Creek along Camp Creek all the way down to the Verde River just below Bartlett Dam. The nearest town is Carefree.

Canada Del Oro Placers

The placers run the headwaters of the Canyon to almost Oracle. The nearest large city is Tucson.

The Cave Creek Placers

These placers are located along Cave Creek just north of Carefree. The creek takes Southwest turn from the south. The placers are on the eastside of the turn. The nearest town is Cave Creek.

Dos Cabezas Placers

These placers form a horseshoe around the town of Dos Cabezas. The horse would have been walking east.

Dripping Springs Placers

These placers are located on a short section of Dripping Springs Creek just east of Kelvin. Highway 77 makes an "S" turn to the east of the placers. The gold is nearer the top part of the "S". The nearest large city is Superior.

Gila City Placers

$500,000 worth of gold was washed from these placers by 1865. These placers are located along the Gila River from where Highway 95 crosses the river to about 2 miles past the city of Dome.

Globe Placers.

These placers run a short distance to the south out of Globe along the west side of Highway 7.

Greaterville Placers

These placers run parallel to highway 82 from Patagonia to Nogales.

Harquahala Mines Gold Rush

The easiest way to get there is to travel northeast on highway 60/70 from where I-10 intersects. When you reach a small town of Salome you want to catch a road headed south into the Little Harquahala Mountains. The Placers are located about midway between Salome and I-10.

The Hassayampa River

Look between Highway 60/70 to the Gila River crossing. The largest city is Wickenburg.

Huachuca Placers

This placer produced a nugget valued at $450 when gold was $32 an ounce. These placers are located just west of the south to east bend of highway 92. Some of the placers are in the Coronado National Memorial. The nearest large town is Bisbee to the East.

The Kofa Mountain Placers.

To get to these placers you must on highway 95 between Yuma and Quartzsite. About a mile north of Stone Cabin there is a turn off going to the east headed to King's Valley. There will be a fork in the road to the north. Take it. The placers are located to the west of Saw Tooth Peak and south of Polaris Mountain. There are several large mines in the area.

La Cholla Placers

These placers are located about 8 miles southwest of Quartzsite along the foot hills of the Dome Rock Mountains. Unfortunately this is part of the Yuma Proving grounds and it is a restricted area. To get to these placers, you will have to obtain permission from the US Army. Good luck!

Laguna Dam Placers

During the construction of the Laguna Dam, there was a placer uncovered along with a small gold vein. There are several small placers along the east bank of the Laguna Reservoir.

La Pas Placers

The first party to discover this area priced up $8000 of nuggets in 1862. Unfortunately most of the placers are on an Indian Reservation. But, there are some of the placers Near I-10, south of the Ghost Town of La Pas. There are two canyons running parallel to I-10 which intersect the Colorado River. The placers are at the headwaters of these canyons. The more southern canyon has a tributary, which branches to the southeast. At the point where I-10 crosses this canyon, is the location of another small placer. Another small placer is crossed by I-10 about 8 miles west of Quartzsite.

Lynx Creek

Along highway 69 you can pan only. Make sure you pay attention to any signs or posted restrictions. This area is just east of Prescott. This area is open to panning to the public. However, it is panning only!

Palmosa Placers

These placers are located about 5 miles south east of Quartzsite. To get to the area, take the primitive road coming off 95 about 3 miles due south of Quartzsite.

The Quijotoa Placers

These placers are located directly south of Quijotoa southeast of highway 86.

Rich Hill Placers

Rich hill was found in 1863 by Major Peeples. It was a hill that use to be a part of the Hassayampa River bed. This hill allowed Major Peeples to pick up $7000 in gold nuggets before he was called to breakfast. Rich Hill is located just west of Stanton and the placers run south along the north fork of the Hassayampa River all the way to Wickenburg.

The San Domingo Placers.

These placers are dry. A dry washer is necessary to do these placers. Or you can transport the dirt to water and use your Highbanker or sluice box. The Placers are found between Morristown and Chamiie. The largest city in the area is Wickenburg.

The Sunflower Placers.

The location of these placers is a bit harder to find unless you are familiar with the area. They are located on Sycamore Creek just south of Sunflower. Highway 87 will be running on the westside of the creek, and the creek will be in a deep section of the canyon.

Tank Mountain Dry Placers

These placers are at the headwaters running out of the Tank Mountains near the north tip of the Yuma Proving Grounds (US Army) north of highway 8. There are no major roads into this area. The only way to reach it is up the dry wash, which intersects the Gila River between Aztec and Sentenel along Highway 8

.

Teviston Dry Placers

Just south of Highway 10, just west of Bowie. These placers are on the east side of the Dos Cabezas Mountains. The nearest town is to the west and this is Wilcox.

Trigo Placers

These placers run parallel to each other just south of Ehrenberg. One of the washes is believed to be Mohave Wash. The other is just north of that. These placers extend to the east of the Colorado River into the Yuma Proving ground. Make sure you pay attention to the restricted area signs. However, there is about two miles between the Colorado River and the Proving Grounds restricted area.

The Vulture Mine Placers.

The Vulture Mine produced $17 million before it was shut down. The Placers are just to the north of the mine near Wickenburg.

CALIFORNIA

Gold Country—These placers are in the Sierra Nevadas and are too numerous to try to give directions individually. However, I will work my way north along the Sierra Nevada Range.

Chowchilla River-north fork of the headwaters Mariposa Creek—upper half of river and headwaters Merced River—headwaters Hornitos—Surrounding area around the town.

Don Dedro Resevour—from dam down stream for about 1 mile. And, above the reservoir long the Tuolumne River about 10 miles. Dogtown Placers— Along west side of highway 395 about 8 miles south of Bridgeport.

Monoville Placers—north of Mono Lake near highway 395

Tulloch Dam—Extends about 10 miles below the dam, and the tributaries feeding the lake

Angels Camp—most major streams in the area.

New Hogan Reservoir—Both main tributaries which feed the lake

Mokelumne River—headwaters

Yuba River—Head waters above Smartsville

Feather River—all major tributaries that feed the lake behind Oroville
Dam

Butte Creek—Headwaters above Chico

DryCreek—headwaters

Cosumnes River—headwaters and most major tributaries. The American River—All headwaters to include the south fork, middle fork, and the north fork, plus all major tributaries which feed these rivers.

Oreg Creek—headwaters

North Fork of the Yuba River—all the way to Sierra City.

Dry Creek

Cottonwood Creek

Clear Creek

The Trinity River—Most feeding tributaries to include the south fork.

The Salmon River—all branches

Wooley Creek

Indian Creek

The Smith River—all forks

The Kalmath River—along with most major tributaries, and above where it crosses highway 96.

Notice: The following placers are not as numerous as those in the Sierra Nevadas or Northern California. Therefore, I tried to give some directions as to how to locate them.

Ballena Placers

These placers run parallel to highway 78 from Ramona east about 10 miles. The canyon with the placers is on the south side of the road.

Coolgardie

This placer is almost due north of Barstow. In fact, the road goes north out of Barstow towards Opal Mountain. The gold will be on the south side of the mountain.

Dale Mining District

There are a couple of mines in the local area along with the placers. This area produced over $1, 000, 000 in gold between 1900 and 1915. The placers are dry. The location is about twenty miles east of Twentynine Palms, just north of the Joshua Tree National Monument.

Goldstone

These placers are due north of Barstow. Catch the road going north out of Barstow and head for the dry lakes. The gold will be south east of the dry lakes.

Holcomb Valley Placers

Also known as the Golden Frenzy of 1860. Holcomb Valley is about half way between Big Bear Lake and Lugerne Valley. There is a small road which takes off from the main road on the north side of Big Bear Lake which will take you into the valley.

Julian Wash

This wash empties into the Colorado River. It is located about 10 miles northeast of Picacho at the top of a big bend in the Colorado River. None of my maps show a road going into this area. Therefore, it might be a good one to 4 wheel into someday.

Kelso Valley Placers

The main body of this placer is in Claraville and north about one mile. the second is northeast of the first about two miles. This area is approximately 50 miles due east of Bakersfield.

Kern River Placers

These Placers are along the Kern River below Isabella Lake. There are two small tributaries below the dam which also contain placer deposits. The river runs along the north side of highway 178 out of East Bakersfield. The Placers die out about half way between the dam and Bakersfield.

Lockwood Valley Placers

This area lies between I-5 and highway 33. The turn off to get to the area is on I-5 at Lebec. Just west of Frazier Park the road takes a fork, both going to highway 33. You want the south fork. It will take you to a creek which will run parallel to the road all the way to highway 33. This is the creek that contains the placers.

Lucas Canyon Placers

These placers are located about halfway between Elsinore and Highway 5. The canyon runs roughly parallel to the road.

Mesquite Dry Placers

Highway 78 cuts across these placers, and they are at the southeast corner of the Chocolate Mountains Aerial Gunnery Range. Make sure you keep your eyes open for any restricted area signs.

Navajo and Placer Creek Placers

There are three areas where these placers exist. The first is right on the edge of La Panza and extends south about ½ mile. The second is approximately 2 miles east of La Panza on highway 58. The road makes a round hump around the placer. The third is about three miles west on highway 58 from the 2nd placer. These are small placers. Blink and you'll probably miss them

.

Piru Creek

This creek runs east west and intersects Pyramid Lake near I-5. This area is bout fifty miles northwest of Los Angeles along I-5.

San Francisquito Canyon

The canyon lies between highway 99 and highway 14 just North of Saugus. There are two other placers in the same area. These are Texas Canyon and Bouquet Canyon.

Santa Felicia Canyon Placers

These placers are on the east side of Piru Lake running east toward I-5. Los Angeles is about 20 miles to the southeast, and the nearest junction is I-5 and highway 126.

Summit Diggings

Just north of Red Mountain (a town), highway 395 makes a hump around the diggings. Also, there is a small placer on the outskirts (north side) of Randsburg. Golpher Gulch abd Black Mountain Placers are east of the Diggings at about 3 and 6 miles respectively. On the east side of Garlock (a ghost town) is another small placer. All of these are located between highway 395 and highway 14 south of China Lake.

Tujunga Canyon Placers

This area is the old Gold District of 1843 and includes Placerita and Saint Peak placers. This area is between Pasadena and Saugus running parallel to I-5, and east of Pasadena to Azusa. This also takes in the San Gavriel Canyon Placers directly north of Azusa. Willow Creek Placers. This area is right along side highway 1, about halfway between San

Simeon and Big Sur

COLORADO

The Arkansas River

This placer runs from the headwaters of the Arkansas River near Leadville to Salida. Highway 24 parallels the river in most places. The tributaries that feed gold into the Arkansas from Leadville south to Salida are :

Coronado Gulch

Halfmoon Creek

Box Creek

Lake Creek

Cache Creek

Clear Creek

Pine Creek

Cottonwood Creek

Chalk Creek

All of these have produced gold in every five gallon bucket full of dirt. It is interesting that all of these creeks come in to the Arkansas from the West. Don't bother with the creeks coming in from the east with the exception of Empire Creek (just south of Leadville).

Clear Creek Placers

These placers take in Chicago Creek, the west and middle branches of Clear Creek from Central City to Golden. This is a fairly large area, but some parts are off limits due to claims and private land. Pay close attention to claim markers and posted signs.

Hahns Peak Placers

These placers run along the west side of the highway running through Hahns Peak of about a mile on either side of the town. The nearest large town is Steamboat Springs to the southeast.

Fairplay Placers

These placers run northeast out of Fairplay on the headwaters of the South Platte River (this includes both forks).

Swan River Placers

The gold runs from the fork of Swan river to the headwaters, and all around the east side of Breckenridge.

Tarryall Placers

The gold extends from highway 285 up Tarryall Creek headwaters (both forks).

Tincup Placers

These placers are located in the creek running from Tincup to the Tayor Resevour. This area is rough, high country. A four wheel drive is a must.

Washington Gulch Placers

These placers are located about two miles northwest of Crested Butte along Slade River.

BIBLIOGRAPHY

1. Barns, Will, C. ARIZONA PLACE NAMES, The University of Arizona Press, Tucson, 1960.

2. Funk and Wagnalls New Encyclopedia, Funk and Wagnalls, Inc., New York, 1983

3. Sheridan, Michael and Jan. RECREATIONAL GUIDE TO THE SUPERSTITION MOUNTAINS AND SALT RIVER LAKES, Impression Makers, Tempe, 1984.

4. United States Department of Agriculture, MINING IN NATIONAL FORESTS, Forest Service, Washington DC, 1982.

5. Waite, Mitchell. THE LOST DUTCHMAN'S NEWSLETTERS, VOLUME I, JUNE 1989 THROUGH MAY 1990, Southwest Publications, Colorado Springs, Co, 1991

6. Waite, Mitchell. THE LOST DUTCHMAN'S NEWSLETTERS, VOLUME II, JUNE 1990 THROUGH MAY 1991, Southwest Publications, Colorado Springs, Co, 1992.

7. Robert Neil Johnson, GOLD DIGGERS ATLAS, Cy Johnson and Son, Susanville, Ca 96130, 1971.

ABOUT THE AUTHOR

Mitch Waite has been a life-time prospector working the gold fields of Arizona, California, and Colorado. He learned from the best of the ole' timers using the equipment they built themselves. Mitch took these concepts and adapted new designs to improve the efficiency of the various gold extraction equipment.

CPSIA information can be obtained at www.ICGtesting.com
Printed in the USA
240501LV00005B/1/P